30-Minute Guide To Hiring A Great Online Marketing Company

7 Hard Truths Every CEO Needs to Know That Only Another CEO Can Tell You

ISBN: 978-1514716977

Copyright © Grow Team 2015

Published by Grow Team Inc., California, USA

First edition published June 2015

All Rights Reserved. No part of this book may be reproduced or utilized in any form or by any means, electronic or mechanical, including photocopying, recording, or by any information storage and retrieval system, without written permission from the publisher.

Why we wrote this book

As entrepreneurs ourselves, we have a very personal connection to the challenges of growing a business and understand how much a bad partnership can affect a company. We've spent years in our own businesses learning the market, hiring vendors, firing vendors, making money, losing money and struggling to keep up with the rapidly changing landscape of online marketing and e-commerce. We have also struggled with deciding when to hire internal staff or outsource and how to effectively manage contractors and their work.

Driven by our frustrations with these sorts of challenges, we came together in 2013 and founded Grow Team, the first national quality and performance vetting service for online marketing companies. Our idea was simple: find the best marketing agencies in the country, help companies get great deals with them and make sure they perform on the back-end. Since inception, Grow Team's experts have evaluated and thoroughly vetted more than 3,000 online marketing companies and helped hundreds of small and medium-sized businesses contract with them for services. We are the first true buyer's agency for online marketing services and have been growing our national presence at a rapid pace.

This book is our way of sharing the knowledge and experience we've gained from negotiating hundreds of online marketing service contracts with a large group of business owners.

People often ask us: "Doesn't giving away your knowledge undermine your business?" Definitely not. By telling people about what we do and sharing our experience, we will certainly help some people manage this process for themselves, but we will also inspire a lot of other people to call us and ask us to help them improve their businesses and take advantage of the thousands of hours of work we've already put into researching and negotiating these kinds of contracts. Either way, we are furthering our mission of helping business owners become more educated buyers of online marketing services.

Why "Hard Truths?"

In the course of starting and running our own companies, we have learned some difficult lessons. The most important of these we call Hard Truths. As a CEO you get a lot of advice: from employees, investors, advisors and vendors; but rarely from people that have had to do your job. This book contains truths about succeeding online that haven't always been easy to accept but have ultimately been the foundation for our success.

Hard Truth Number One: You won't succeed long term without outside help

In our practice, we work with hundreds of CEOs and understand that everyone has their own opinion about the relative value of outsourcing vs staffing internally. Most business owners make an effort to staff up internally around functions that they perceive to be core competencies of the business. This logic generally works well, as full-time employees give you more control and oversight on their work, as well as a better opportunity to retain the accumulated knowledge from that work if they ever leave or are terminated.

If you operate a business that depends on the Internet for a substantial portion of your leads and revenue, it is easy to extend this basic thinking to online marketing functions. Depending on the size of your company and the amount of revenue coming from online efforts, you may have a single person managing your site and campaigns or a small team of internal people. While it may make sense in very large companies to completely in-source online marketing support, for the vast majority of businesses it simply isn't the best strategy. There are three reasons successful companies outsource to compete online:

Rapid platform evolution

The platforms on which you market your products and services (Google, Facebook, LinkedIn, etc.) and the entry points to them (paid ads, content, re-targeting, mobile apps, etc.) are evolving and changing at a rapid pace. Best practices, strategies and ad programs are becoming increasingly complex and specialized, requiring more time and effort to stay competent from an administrative point of view. Lack of awareness or involvement in new programs can also mean lost opportunity and lost revenue.

Accelerated training requirements

Because of the rapid changes in the platforms themselves, the amount of training required to stay at the top of the game is increasing dramatically. The amount of time one person would have to spend getting trained and staying current on all the various aspects of online marketing would easily eat up their entire week and leave no time to actually do the work you hired them to do. Professional marketing firms can spread the cost and utilization of this kind of training across a broad set of clients, making it feasible – whereas you simply cannot.

The use of specialized software

As the platforms and marketing channels continue to evolve, the need to monitor brand assets, coordinate content and optimize ad buying across those channels is becoming more critical. Many agencies have developed specialized software to aid them in these processes, or pay large licensing fees to use commercially available tools, giving their clients an edge over less sophisticated competitors. The use of these applications is often not possible or prohibitively expensive for many small businesses.

Hard Truth Number Two: Winners focus on ROI - not cost

This is probably the biggest mistake CEOs make: starting their evaluation process and outlining their budget before they've defined their needs or what constitutes success for them. They start the discussion with vendors by saying, "I have a budget of $X a month; what can you do for me?" Then they get answers from the vendors and decide who they think is the best choice.

Successful owners start by asking the right questions:

Power Questions:

- What will it take to increase my sales online by X% over the next 12 months?

- Given my size/position related to my competitors, how much do we really need to invest to effectively compete? In which areas (SEO, paid search, affiliate, social, mobile, etc.?) should we be focusing our investment?

- Given my product/service set, current positioning and budget, what are the highest ROI activities we should be focusing on?

- How can we ensure that as we go down the road, we quickly eliminate non-performing activities and focus our dollars on profitable ones? What metrics should we use to identify them?

- What is a reasonable expectation of overall ROI for the investment I'm making?

Those are the kinds of questions that will lead to a blueprint for success, rather than simply a list of things that will be done for a given budget.

Playing to win

The reason this is important is because people often wonder why they don't get the results that they want. Generally, this is because they aren't asking the right questions. They focus on a budget figure rather than getting an accurate picture of what investment is needed to create positive ROI. You are competing directly against other companies that are investing in the same kinds of services, so understanding where you need to be positioned relative to them is critical. Many companies fail because they invest too little or try to take on major competitors with too little ammunition. Great vendors will tell you when you're under-sizing the task, but there are always people willing to take your money and give you false hope that you can succeed, when really they know you can't.

Another aspect of making a smart investment in online marketing services is allowing for additional costs on your end to support the work the vendor is doing. You may need to spend additional staff time to augment their efforts and implement their recommendations. It's important to factor these costs into your overall budget as well as your ROI calculations, so that you get a true sense of the return. The right way to think about it is: "What do I need to invest in a program so that I win? So that I become relevant enough to attract clients and build significant ROI?

Let's say you were going to enter a marathon and were talking to a trainer and you said, "I want you to train me for the marathon but I'm only willing to spend two hours a week training." A trainer who is desperate for the money and doesn't really care will say, "OK, sure. I'll work with you for two hours. I will put together a plan and we can get started next week." On the other hand, someone who really knows what they're doing will look at you and say, "You might as well not waste your time, because you'll never even finish the race if you don't commit at least 10 hours a week to the training process – and I don't coach people that won't finish."

We have a client who runs a professional services firm and when they first came to us, they were doing about $1,000,000 a year in online sales. Sales had been flat for over a year and they were looking for ways to move the needle and increase revenue. When we spoke to them originally, we talked to them about what they were trying to accomplish (their campaigns, etc.) and the CEO was adamant that he wasn't willing to increase his budget. They had a vendor in place that had been working with them for the last two years and he felt that the amount that he was investing was an amount that he wasn't willing to increase.

We really got into a deep conversation about what his objectives were and as we really defined his goals for growth, it became very clear to us that he needed a different kind of partner. He needed a partner that could do more comprehensive work than the company that he was with currently and that that work was going to be more expensive. In fact, it was going to be almost double the budget that he was currently spending.

The conversation really turned to ROI vs budget. Over the course of these conversations, we were convinced that he could see significant increases in sales by adopting a different strategy with a different partner, but it would require an additional investment. Ultimately, he took our advice and decided to go with the company that we recommended. The additional cost was $3,000/month over what he was paying before, but with the new program in place his sales tripled. If you figured it on an ROI basis it was almost a 900% return - obviously a win for him, but would never have happened if he'd stuck with a fixed budget.

Hard Truth Number Three: A bad contract guarantees failure

After negotiating hundreds of online marketing contracts, we've identified two areas that are most often responsible for bad contract relationships:

Lack of specific service deliverables

Depending on the type of service you are contracting for, there are usually a set of specific deliverables associated with it: amount of content to be created, pages optimized, affiliates created, budget spent, etc. Throughout the sales process, the person on the agency side will talk about these things, so it's critical to make notes on them and then make sure they are included in the actual contract. This is really on the owner, since a lot of companies default to leaving this kind of detail out of contracts so that they have more wiggle room down the road.

Power Questions:

- How can I quantify the work that you are doing? What specific work and/or activity is expected to be done every month?

- After the first phase of implementation, what are the things that I'm going to be receiving on an ongoing basis?

Lack of specific communication expectations

This is a big one. How often will they talk to you? In our experience, the best companies out there have regular, planned communication with clients which allows them to update you on progress and learn about any new developments on your end that may impact what they're doing. Agencies who say they are there "when you need them" or that communication "depends on what's going on that month" may be sincere, but being specific up-front sets the tone for a productive long term relationship and creates a clear expectation that can be referenced if there are problems with the account manager later on.

Power Questions:
- Who will I be talking with on a regular basis and how often will we be communicating?

- What should my team prepare for these scheduled calls to make them more productive? What information from our end would be helpful?

Hard Truth Number Four: You go to bed with the salesperson but wake up with the account manager

Falling in love with the salesperson

Some of the worst companies in this space have the best sales people.

They know exactly what to say and are excellent at selling the big brands and major experience of their firm. In the sales process, they will promote that they work with Honda, Nike, IBM, etc. and dazzle you with their experience and white papers, most of which are about companies much bigger than yours, i.e. the ones that they put their really smart account managers on. If you focus on this aspect of their pitch, you'll probably be thinking "Wow, these guys must be really good. After all, Honda wouldn't work with schmucks."

They build rapport and confidence with you and convince you that everyone on their team will be just as good as they are and care deeply about your account. Now, we're not knocking legitimate salespeople and the work they do, but a lot of companies in the online marketing space have adopted a business model that specifically focuses their resources on sales at the direct expense of service, because they believe it is cheaper to acquire new clients than it is to retain them. This is the "churn-and-burn" model at its best (or worst). This is why we strongly recommend vetting the actual account manager before signing a contract, because when all is said and done, they are the one you will be dependent on for results.

The importance of account manager selection

As part of the build-out of our national network, we have evaluated thousands of companies and hundreds of individual account managers within those companies. We went into the online marketing companies and actually invested the time to understand the account management structure and its impact on performance. Here's what we learned.

99% of the success of your relationship with an online marketing company will be determined by your specific account manager. What often happens is that when the sales manager closes a new account, it goes into a lottery system for account manager assignment based on which of their staff have the most availability. And guess who usually has the most availability? Newer, less experienced account managers who don't already have a full book of clients. This is especially true if you are a small business client in a large agency.

Account managers drive your experience and results

It may seem obvious to say that not all account managers are created equal, but our experience has been that most companies have very little formal, ongoing training or fixed procedures related to the communication cycles and work which account managers put into individual accounts. This results in an extremely high correlation between campaign performance and individual project manager assignment.

After evaluating the performance of hundreds of campaigns, we found that account managers who consistently ranked at the top end of the scale not only increased the performance of the campaigns they were responsible for, but also retained their clients longer. Communication was more frequent, follow-up was better and clients were generally happier.

So how do you get a good account manager?

Ask for one. More specifically, tell the vendor that you need to know who your account manager will be before you sign a contract. Talk to them, interview them and look up their background. What are their values? What's their skill set? What's their experience? Ask them specific questions about your website and what their plan is to help you improve it. If you don't like the answers, ask for a different account manager up front.

Power Questions:

- What experience do you have with the specific services I'm contracting for?

- What training or certifications do you have?

- Have you worked on similar-sized accounts in the past?

- What is your plan to increase revenue for my business? Why?

- What's the best way for us to communicate?

What if you think you have a bad account manager?

Demand to switch. You should do this immediately. Wasting time trying to make a bad account manager better isn't your problem - it's a training issue that the vendor needs to address.

You should never be shy about calling the senior manager at a vendor and asking for a new account rep if you're not happy.

The big lesson here is that it's fine to evaluate the company you're going to contract with, but if you don't evaluate them down to the individual account manager, you are risking the performance of your entire campaign. Don't be dazzled by their client list, white papers and PowerPoint decks - focus on the people that will actually be doing the work for you.

Hard Truth Number Five: Bad companies don't come with warning labels

Like most things in business, you get a gut feeling for whether the things that your vendors are doing are legitimate and are being done right. You don't need to be a technical expert, but you do need to know enough to know when you're getting scammed. Here are some red flags to look for and how you can identify trouble before it gets too far down the line.

Lack of Transparency

The first red flag is lack of transparency. This takes many forms, such as when a vendor says that they're creating content for you but they won't show it to you. They may reference articles or blogs that they've created but won't send you copies for review and approval. They may make changes to the actual content on your site but not offer you detail on what changes were made and when. Some will even claim that they've built links to your site without disclosing which sites they are on, saying that it's part of their "proprietary process".

Access to Accounts

Access to accounts is another dangerous red flag. If a vendor says that they've created accounts for you - especially Google AdWords accounts or other advertising accounts – but they won't give you access to them, you should be worried. They may tell you that they are managing them under their "internal system" or as part of their "master account" and can't give you access - don't believe them. If you're paying for third party ad services, you need access and control over those accounts; not just to monitor the money, but to retain the valuable intelligence from historical data in the account if you ever fire the vendor.

Bogus Reporting

The third area of common abuse is reporting. There are reporting platforms which are specifically designed to allow vendors to create confusing reports that mask a lack of performance. SEO is an area where this is most often abused, and we often see vendors sending out reports that are either intentionally confusing or outright fabrications. The bottom line is that you are smart enough to understand any report that's legitimate. Don't be intimidated to ask questions and make them explain every part of the reporting to you… and if the explanation doesn't make sense to you, there's probably a reason.

We had a client come to us and say: "I think my marketing company is doing a good job, but I'm just not seeing the sales increases I should be." When we asked why he thought that, he showed us a report from the vendor showing that he had had 65 "conversions" on his paid search campaign last month, which the vendor said were completed sales from clients who had clicked through on paid ads. "But the number of sales on the site last month was only 43 in total," he explained. "I just don't know why things aren't adding up; I mean, the numbers from Google can't be wrong, can they?"

So we called the vendor and started asking direct questions about the "conversions" tracking they were doing and also asked for access to the AdWords account. It turned out that there were some "mistakes" which had been made with the tracking pixels and that the real conversion numbers were much lower. They couldn't explain exactly what the mistakes were or why they had been reporting numbers which didn't match up to the actual Google Analytics for months.

Needless to say, this vendor relationship was short-lived and we got the client into a relationship with a reputable company. He now understands his reports clearly and can match them up with real sales every month.

The bad apples

Like any market, this one has bad apples. Unlike other markets, they can be a lot harder to spot.

The fact is that there are a lot of churn-and-burn companies which spend all of their energy strategizing around how to sell, mislead and retain you with little or no focus on actual performance. The really bad ones actively engage in tactics and practices that can be harmful to your business in the long term.

Getting on the right side

The long-term strategy for your business online should be based on best practices and on alignment with the interests of the platforms upon which you are advertising. If you ask the right high-level questions, they will lead you to the right conclusions: "Does the strategy we're pursuing benefit the end user?" "Does it make for a better experience for the person coming to the search engine or the website?" If you maintain focus on these questions, it's easy to tell when someone is recommending something that might get you in trouble down the road.

Ethical companies attract ethical employees and will talk about things like alignment, best practices and guidelines. They don't use words like gaming, tricking or masking and don't suggest that you create junk content or engage in partnerships with affiliates which aren't above board. They don't make lofty promises and they don't make guarantees about things they don't control. Avoid the temptation of things that sound too good to be true; focus on the right questions and listen to your gut.

Bonus Content

To get a free checklist of the 15 critical questions every owner should ask when evaluating an outside marketing vendor, please go to

www.growteam.com/questions

Hard Truth Number Six: The worst advice comes with good intentions

Good intentions, bad advice

As you evolve your business strategy over time, you have to be conscious of who you're asking for advice. If you're working with a firm which is heavily geared towards social media marketing, they're likely to believe that the thing you should be spending your money on going forward is, unsurprisingly, more social media. The same thing would be true with a pay-per-click company, an SEO company, an affiliate marketing company and so on. Given this truth, it's critical that you find ways to get input from people who don't have a vested interest in one specific type of service or marketing platform.

It's important for business owners to get some outside opinions about the total strategy that they wish to implement. Just asking their vendors how they should be approaching things is clearly not enough, because the vendors are obviously biased towards the types of services that they provide. It's not out of malice; it's purely because that's what they know. That's what they believe in, otherwise they wouldn't be in that line of work.

Aside from specific vendor bias, it's also important to be aware that the market is constantly changing. In earlier chapters we talked about ROI being the metric that's most important. As you track ROI, it is often the case that as the months go on, certain types of activities will start to drive higher ROI than others. It may be in your best interest to move investment dollars from one type of activity to another. Unfortunately, if it means losing a contract, most vendors won't be eager to highlight that to you.

Search for the highest ROI use of funds

As the owner, your question shouldn't be: "Can I make positive ROI on this activity?" The power question is:

"Is this activity the highest ROI activity available to me right now?"

Those are very different questions. If you're asking the latter question, it forces you to look at everything and evaluate the potential returns that you could be getting. If you're asking a vendor or someone who is specifically involved in one aspect of online marketing, they're very likely to tell you that they think that the thing that they do most often is the answer... which it may not be. This is also a question which should be asked broadly in the business and put up against other offline marketing opportunities like print and direct sales.

One of our clients is an e-commerce specialty products company that came to us spending five figures a month on pay-per-click ads and $3,500 a month on an SEO company which was doing content marketing work for them. We looked at the overall investment that they were making, the performance of their campaigns and their blended cost of traffic. We ended up recommending that they reallocate their content marketing budget into a contract with a new vendor for a special type of technical SEO work and restructure their paid search program. The result of those changes was that organic traffic increased 35% in 90 days, representing an additional $30,000 a month in sales. By lowering their blended cost of acquisition overall, they were able to be more competitive with their paid search campaigns as well, expanding their reach into new ad networks and increasing ROI.

Getting quality outside advice and perspective on your marketing programs can be a challenge, but is well worth the effort.

a call with the CEO will trigger him/her to review your campaigns, get a status update from their team and make everyone downstream aware that you are directly communicating with the boss. It also gives you visibility at the top and puts you front-of-mind with the senior executive who may have other introductions or recommendations that could benefit you.

About the Authors

Derek Preston

Derek Preston is the 2011 "CEO of the Year" award winner, veteran entrepreneur and passionate advocate for performance and accountability in vendor relationships. His unique experience helps business owners create winning market strategies, find the best partners and deliver return on investment.

- 2011 CEO of the Year, Entrepreneurs Organization, San Diego
- Raised $22 million in investment capital for his companies
- Founded, funded and sold four companies in the last 20 years

Derek and his companies have been featured in the *Wall Street Journal*, *Consumer Reports* and the *New York Times*, as well as on CNN, ABC and CNBC.

Originally from Michigan, Derek lives in San Diego with his wife and two children. He enjoys adventure travel and donates his time to several non-profit and business mentoring groups.

www.linkedin.com/in/derekpreston

Brian Moaddeli

Brian Moaddeli is a senior executive with experience in all aspects of early stage company growth, including building revenue strategies and operational processes. His experience includes recruiting, training and managing over 500 salespeople and 1,000 outside contractors. He has founded, funded and sold three companies in the last 15 years.

He has a broad base of experience in negotiating and managing contracts with outside suppliers, focused on generating long-term performance and results.

Brian lived in Toronto, moved to Chicago and then to San Diego. He currently lives there with his wife and is actively involved in the entrepreneurial community in the city. He has served on the board of the Entrepreneur's Organization in San Diego, as well as volunteering as a mentor through their small businesses Accelerator program. He has travelled to over 30 countries.

https://www.linkedin.com/in/brianmoaddeli

Want a Free Assessment?

We help companies find the best online marketing partners at the best price. If you'd like us to evaluate your website and tell you what we think, just give us a call and tell us that you read our book.

Grow Team Main Office

800-741-9298

Or Visit

www.GrowTeam.com

Made in the USA
Middletown, DE
23 November 2016